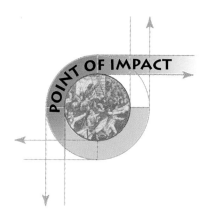

POINT OF IMPACT

The Fall of the Bastille

Revolution in France

STEWART ROSS

Heinemann Library
Chicago, Illinois

Customer Service 888-454-2279

Visit our website at www.heinemannlibrary.com

Produced for Heinemann Library by Discovery Books Limited
Designed by Ian Winton
Illustrations by Stefan Chabluk
Printed in Hong Kong

05 04 03 02
10 9 8 7 6 5 4 3 2

Library of Congress Cataloging-in-Publication Data

Ross, Stewart.
    The fall of the Bastille : revolution in France / Stewart Ross.
        p. cm.
    Includes bibliographic references and index.
    ISBN 1-58810-076-6
    1. Bastille--Juvenile literature. 2. France--History--Revolution,
1789-1799--Juvenile literature. [1. Bastille. 2. France--History--Revolution, 1789-1799.]
I. Title.
DC167 .R677 2001
944.04--dc21
                          00-011701

Acknowledgments
The Publishers would like to thank the following for permission to reproduce photographs:
Mary Evans, pp. 4, 7, 9, 10, 11, 13, 15, 26; The Art Archive, pp. 5, 12, 14, 21; Peter Newark's Historical Pictures, pp. 6, 8, 24, 25, 28; Hulton-Deutsch Collection, pp. 16, 17, 22; Hulton Getty, pp. 18, 19, 23; Peter Newark's Military Pictures, p. 29.

Cover photographs reproduced with the permission of The Art Archive

Every effort has been made to contact copyright holders of any material reproduced in this book. Any omissions will be rectified in subsequent printings if notice is given to the Publisher.

Some words are shown in bold, **like this.** You can find out what they mean by looking in the glossary.

Contents

Revolution!

Siege

The Marquis de Launay, commander of the Bastille, was faced with a difficult problem. He had only 114 men to defend his ancient fortress-prison and its huge stockpiles of gunpowder. Beyond the walls was a mob of over 1,000 Parisians intent on seizing the ammunition. De Launay had ordered his troops to fire on them. Now the enraged mob had two cannons trained on the Bastille's raised wooden drawbridge.

Surrender

De Launay had three options: continue fighting, surrender, or blow up the gunpowder. The cannons aimed at the drawbridge meant certain defeat for the defenders if he decided to fight it out. His own men wouldn't let him set off the gunpowder. There was only one option left. A note was passed through a hole in the drawbridge that said the Bastille would surrender!

Within a few minutes, the mob had rushed in to claim its prize and to punish those responsible for the bloodshed. De Launay and his officers would pay for the citizens who were killed at his command.

Triumph of the people

The Bastille fell on July 14, 1789. It was not the beginning of the French Revolution, but it was an important turning point. The Bastille symbolized royal **tyranny.** Its fall marked the victory of ordinary people over King

A guard at the Bastille passes out a note from the Marquis de Launay, saying that the fortress will surrender.

Louis XVI. Tragically, the mob's victory in their attack of the **garrison** set a violent tone for the years immediately following.

The French Revolution changed France forever and had a huge impact on Europe and the rest of the world. As a result, the fall of the Bastille is now seen as one of the most significant events in modern history.

This romantic impression of the fall of the Bastille shows the walls of the fortress as much taller than they really were, to exaggerate the achievement of the attackers.

WHAT IS A REVOLUTION?

A revolution is a rapid, total, and enduring change. The French Revolution was basically a political revolution, although social and economic changes followed it. Other types of revolution include the Industrial Revolution that began in the late eighteenth century and saw the introduction of machines to do work previously been done by hand. As a result, trade, industry, and population all grew at a tremendous rate. More recently, the modern Communications Revolution has brought computers, the Internet, and mobile phones, completely changing the way we work and live.

The Ancien Regime

Three estates

France's government and society before the revolution is known as the **"Ancien Regime."** It was headed by the king. Everyone else belonged to one of three **"Estates."** The First Estate consisted of the **clergy,** the Second Estate was the **nobles,** and the Third Estate was made up of the rest of the population—the ordinary people. Wealthy members of the Third Estate were known as the **bourgeoisie.**

The king, the nobility, and the Catholic Church owned most of the land. Nobles and members of the clergy enjoyed many **privileges,** such as not paying personal taxes. The nobles held many of the best jobs, especially in the army and the Church. Because the whole system was based upon **inherited** rights, it benefited the few at the expense of the many.

Louis XVI, shown here in his coronation robes, inherited great power, although he proved to be an incompetent king.

The causes of the Revolution

The Ancien Regime did not suddenly collapse. Difficulties had been building up for years, and the fall of the Bastille came after a long chain of crises.

The causes of the French Revolution have been endlessly debated. Some historians say it was a class struggle between common people and the privileged groups. Others point to the revolutionary ideas of the "Enlightenment." Also, constant hunger had a role in the uprising by the Third Estate.

The king and queen

Because the king was responsible for running the government, he must take a large share of the blame for what happened. King Louis XVI was well-meaning but lacked the intelligence, good judgment, and strength of character needed for his difficult job. Louis was not helped by his 1770 marriage to the Austrian princess Marie Antoinette. Instead of helping him, she annoyed both **courtiers** and ordinary people with her tactless comments and behavior. She was also an obstacle in ministers' attempts to control France's finances.

Louis XIV built the palace of Versailles outside Paris at the end of the seventeenth century. He used it when he wanted to separate himself and his court from the troublesome Paris crowds.

ROYAL WEAKNESS

A year before the fall of the Bastille, the king's sister, Madame Elizabeth, remarked how her brother seemed incapable of making a firm decision and sticking to it, saying: *"The king is back-tracking. He is always afraid of making mistakes. Once he has made a decision, he is terrified that he might have got it wrong. I believe that in government, as in education, one should not say 'Let it be done' until one is sure of being right."*

The Burden of Debt

Bankruptcy

In the end, Louis XVI's government collapsed because it was **bankrupt.** This was not because France was poor—it was one of the richest countries in Europe. The problem was that for many years the government spent more than it earned. To make up the difference, it borrowed. When Louis XVI came to the throne in 1774, he **inherited** a debt of four billion **livres.**

The government paid **interest** on the money it borrowed. To pay this interest, it borrowed more. Therefore it had to pay more interest, and so the cycle continued. In 1789 the government was spending 300 million livres—more than half its income—in interest. This debt was made worse by France's involvement in the American Revolution from 1775 to 1783.

Reform

There were two ways out of the government's difficulty: either reduce spending or increase income. Under Louis XVI's feeble leadership it managed to do neither.

One of the inequalities of the Ancien Regime was that rich nobles did not have to pay some of the heaviest taxes—peasants such as those shown here did.

Most government income came from taxation. There were two types of tax. Indirect taxes, such as **customs duties** and the *gabelle,* or salt tax, were paid by everyone. There were also direct taxes on personal wealth. These were paid by the **peasants** and **bourgeoisie,** but not by the **privileged nobles** or officials. Many people thought this was unfair, especially since most nobles were very well off and the majority of peasants lived in poverty.

Anne-Robert Turgot, Louis XVI's first finance minister, tried to reform the system. When the privileged classes complained about his ideas, he resigned. His successor went on borrowing.

In 1787, finance minister Charles de Calonne discovered that no one would lend the government any more money. As a last resort, he called a meeting of all the country's privileged groups (the Assembly of Notables) and asked them to help. When they refused, it became clear that the **Ancien Regime** was running out of time.

Mᴿ NECKER.

Jacques Necker (1732–1804), who succeeded Charles de Calonne as finance minister, was also unable to do anything about the country's bankruptcy, but he became a popular hero when he asked the king to summon the Estates General.

Representatives of the people

The nearest thing France had to a Congress was the Estates General. This gathering of the three **Estates** had not met since 1614. In its absence, thirteen supreme law courts (known as **Parlements**) claimed they represented the people of France. The most important was the Parlement of Paris. In reality, the Parlements represented only the Church and privileged landowners. This particularly irritated the wealthy bourgeoisie who dominated the Third Estate. They deeply resented their lack of political influence in the governing of France.

Crisis

No way out

With no money, Louis XVI and his government were powerless. The king, while still popular with the masses, had lost the respect of his court. The queen became mixed up in scandal and was very unpopular. The **privileged** classes had refused to help. The **bourgeoisie** did not believe the king wanted reform. And every day the government's debt got bigger.

The Estates General

The Paris **Parlement** managed to persuade people that it could save the country. Not knowing what to do, Louis banished it from the capital in August 1787, recalled it the next month, dismissed it again and, in May 1788, recalled it again.

The Parlement, however, had nothing new to offer. In August 1788, the king bowed to popular pressure and agreed to summon the Estates General the following May. It would be the first time in over 150 years that representatives of the three **Estates** of the realm had met.

The Third Estate

The king's decision to summon the Estates General sparked a new debate. Should the three Estates meet together or separately? And should the Third Estate have the same number of representatives as each of the other two Estates, or a number equal to both of them combined?

XVIIᵉ SIÈCLE.   Règne de Louis XVI.

Queen Marie Antoinette was famously out of touch with the lives of ordinary people. A story spread among the poor that when the Queen heard they had no bread, she replied, "Let them eat cake!" This rumor angered the hungry people of Paris and in October 1789 thousands of women went to Versailles chanting, "Cut the queen's head off!"

Again Louis gave way to popular pressure. Although he overruled Parlement and agreed that the Estates should meet separately, he did accept double representation for the Third Estate. Of the 610 **deputies** elected to the Third Estate, most belonged to the bourgeoisie and represented the views of professionals, such as lawyers, industrialists, merchants, and bankers. Only a handful of them were **peasants.**

Meanwhile, the mood in the country was darkening. Bad harvests had forced up the price of bread. Faced with starvation, the poor of Paris and other cities were on the verge of revolt.

THE PRICE OF BREAD

The main food of most French families was the four-pound loaf of bread. It normally cost eight **sous.** By February 1789, its price in Paris had almost doubled to fifteen sous—more than half the average daily wage of a typical worker. A family of four needed two loaves a day, which many could not afford. One worker asked of representatives of the Third Estate, *"Are they concerned with us? Are they thinking of lowering the price of bread? We haven't eaten anything for two days."*

The beginning of a revolution? The three Estates—**clergy, nobles,** and common people—go in procession to Versailles for the opening of the Estates General.

Enlightenment

New thinking

Over the previous 75 years, **radical** new ideas had spread across Europe. In France, they changed the way many people regarded the **Ancien Regime.** As a result, some people came to believe that even a reformed Ancien Regime was not enough—they wanted a different system altogether.

Reason, rights, and contracts

Historians call the new thinking the "Enlightenment." It held that reason, rather than faith or tradition, was the best guide to how things should be done. Enlightened thinkers like the French philosopher Voltaire (1694–1778) shocked many people by arguing that most religion was just superstition. His followers wanted to abolish the Church's wealth and **privileges.**

Voltaire, whose ideas helped undermine the Ancien Regime, was imprisoned in the Bastille as a young man for attacking the government.

Some enlightened thinkers spoke of the "natural rights" of every human being, which could not be taken away. They included such things as the right not to be imprisoned without a fair trial. Supporters of the Enlightenment agreed with the English thinker John Locke (1632–1704), who said that government should be based on a contract between the governors and the people they governed. If the governors broke this contract by not governing well, the people had a right to replace them. French thinkers like Charles de Montesquieu (1689–1755) and Jean-Jacques Rousseau (1712–1778) spread these ideas in France.

An American example

In 1775, Britain's colonies in North America rebelled against George III because they believed his government had broken its contract with them. The American colonists believed that anyone paying taxes to a ruler should have representation within that ruler's government. The introduction of unpopular taxes in the colonies, without representation in the British Parliament, was one of the triggers of the American Revolution. The rebellion was successful, and the former colonists set up a new nation, the United States of America. Its **republican** system of government was based on the ideas of the Enlightenment.

France fought with the colonies against Britain, and American ideas became very popular in France. The American colonists' revolt against an unfair and unpopular government inspired the people of France to do the same.

THE DECLARATION OF INDEPENDENCE

The American colonists put forth a famous expression of peoples' rights in the *Declaration of Independence* in 1776. Its principles were very different from those of the Ancien Regime:
"We hold these truths to be self-evident, that all men are created equal, that they are endowed by their Creator with certain unalienable rights, that among these are life, liberty, and the pursuit of happiness."

Colonial leaders signed the *Declaration of Independence* in 1776. The actions of the Americans inspired the critics of the Ancien Regime in France.

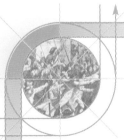

The Third Estate

What is the Third Estate?

Before the **Estates** General met, the king asked people for their opinions and complaints. This resulted in an avalanche of papers and pamphlets offering every kind of opinion. Most took the so-called **"Patriot"** position, calling for an end to **privilege** of the wealthy few. The most influential publication came from the priest Abbé Emmanuel Sieyès and was called *What is the Third Estate?*

A National Assembly

In May 1789, the Estates General met at Versailles, the magnificent royal palace south of Paris. Right away, the **deputies** chosen by the **nobles** and **clergy** voted to assemble in separate chambers. But the deputies representing the Third Estate wanted everyone to meet together. The other Estates refused. So, on June 17, the Third Estate declared that it was a National Assembly representing all of France. It was joined by 150 members of the clergy.

This dramatic painting by artist Jacques-Louis David shows a romanticized view of the Third Estate swearing the famous "tennis court" oath.

Louis XVI now put his foot down and ordered the hall set aside for the Third Estate to be closed. On June 21, the deputies gathered anyway, in a nearby tennis court. They swore not to break up until France had a new, written **constitution.**

Too little, too late

Louis backed down. Two days later he told all the Estates that he would bring in reforms. But he insisted that the three Estates remain separate. It was too little, too late. When a royal official told the Third Estate, or National Assembly, to go to their own hall, they sent him away with the famous words, "*The assembled nation cannot receive orders.*" It was a direct challenge to royal authority.

Louis XVI backed down yet again and told the First and Second Estates to join the National Assembly. Secretly, though, he did not approve of what had happened. While the deputies continued their debate, he ordered 20,000 troops to gather around Paris.

THE POWER OF THE PEN

Before the Estates General met, the visionary priest Abbé Sieyès explained that the Third Estate represented the whole of France. This paved the way for the estate to turn itself into the National Assembly.

"The Third Estate consists of everything that belongs to the nation. And everything outside the Third Estate cannot be seen as part of the nation. So what is the Third Estate? It is the whole of France."

(From *What is the Third Estate?*)

Abbé Emmanuel Sieyès was one of the few leaders to take part in almost every stage of the revolution. By 1799, he had lost his faith in democracy and helped Napoleon come to power.

To Arms!

Royal power

The king said the troops were in the Paris region to keep order and protect the National Assembly. The **deputies** did not believe him. When they asked Louis XVI to remove the troops, he refused.

Most French people backed the Assembly, but actual power remained with the king and his soldiers. So, unless something unusual happened, any hope of revolution was doomed. However, in the second week of July 1789, something unusual did happen.

Simmering violence

The common people of Paris had followed the events at Versailles with great interest. Starving and suspicious of the king and the **nobles,** they saw the National Assembly as their only hope of salvation. They guessed correctly that the troops were gathering to crush the **Patriot** cause. Over the past few months, there had been many violent outbursts as hungry mobs seized grain stores, mills, and bakeries. On July 11, the king fired the popular finance minister, Jacques Necker. When the news reached Paris the next day, the city suddenly erupted.

A revolutionary shoots the royal servant Jacques de Flesselles for misleading the people about where arms were kept.

People power

Stirred up by street-corner **orators** like Camille Desmoulins, the Paris mob went on a rampage. When the army tried to restore order, soldiers siding with the people fought back. Furious citizens armed with stolen weapons tore down government customs posts. A starving crowd attacked the monastery of Saint-Lazare—which was also a food-storage location—and looted grain, wine, and cheese.

A counterattack was expected at any moment. To fight it off, the people needed weapons. They seized a cannon and more than 30,000 rifles from the **Hôtel des Invalides garrison.** But they still had no gunpowder. However, 250 barrels of it were stored in the Bastille, an ancient fortress used as a prison. On the morning of July 14, the mob set off to get it.

I WOULD RATHER DIE!

Camille Desmoulins, speaking outside of the Palais Royal on July 14, urged Parisians to take up arms to defend themselves. *"Now they have forced out Necker, the **privileged** classes will do anything! Maybe tonight they are plotting to massacre the Patriots? To arms! Yes, I summon my brothers to freedom: I would rather die than submit to **servitude**!"*

The writings and speeches of Camille Desmoulins urged the people of Paris to revolt in 1789. He was executed by the revolutionary government in 1794.

The Bastille

By command of the king

Built as a fortress in the late fourteenth century, the Bastille had been used as a prison for the previous 150 years. Most of its prisoners had been detained by command of the king. Some were traitors, others were writers of "dangerous" material, **heretics,** or public nuisances.

This 18th century print of the Bastille shows it as it really was—an old, run-down fortress.

The Bastille had a reputation as a grim place of rat-infested dungeons and torture chambers. In fact, although there were cold and drafty rooms, prisoners who could afford to pay lived quite comfortably, with fires, curtains, and furniture. They were also allowed to bring in their own possessions, food, and drink.

A symbol of tyranny

By 1789 the Bastille had outlived its purpose. It was expensive to maintain and rarely held more than a handful of prisoners. On July 14, 1789, there were only seven.

Whatever the truth was about the Bastille, it was still a hated symbol. Towering over the city, it represented the king's absolute power over his subjects. In the popular imagination it stood for repression, **privilege,**

LETTRES DE CACHET

Most Bastille prisoners were held by a *lettre de cachet*. Written by the king or a government minister, it ordered a victim's instant arrest and imprisonment without trial. By Louis XVI's time, the lettres were very unpopular and the government was considering abolishing them. It also planned to pull down the Bastille and in its place erect a monument with the inscription: *"Louis XVI. Restorer of Public Freedom."*

and **censorship.** So when the cry went up on the morning of July 14—"À bas la Bastille!" ("Down with the Bastille!")— the mob responded with a fiery passion.

The Marquis de Launay, commander of the Bastille, had an extremely difficult job.

LE MARQUIS DE LAUNAY

Gouverneur de la Bastille

Né et mort à Paris, dernier gouverneur de la Bastille, entré en fonctions en 1774; à l'attaque de la forteresse, hésita entre le Roi et le peuple et résista, comptant sur des secours promis. Le peuple, mécontent, l'entraîna à l'hôtel de ville où il fut massacré sur les marches; sa tête fut promenée au bout d'une pique, pendant deux jours, dans les rues de Paris.

Two days' supplies

The Marquis de Launay, commander of the Bastille, was in charge of a **garrison** of 82 retired soldiers aided by 32 Swiss guards. He also had 30 cannons—some positioned along the walls, others in the inner courtyard facing the gate.

But the Bastille was not prepared for a siege. There was no fresh water supply and only enough food for two days. The mob would probably not be able to force their way in, but if relief did not come quickly, de Launay would be forced to surrender.

ive Us the Bastille!

The attack begins

A mob of almost 1,000 people arrived in front of the Bastille. Among them were a few **bourgeoisie** and a handful of soldiers who had changed sides. Most were ordinary citizens, a few of whom thought the Bastille was being used as a food-storage location.

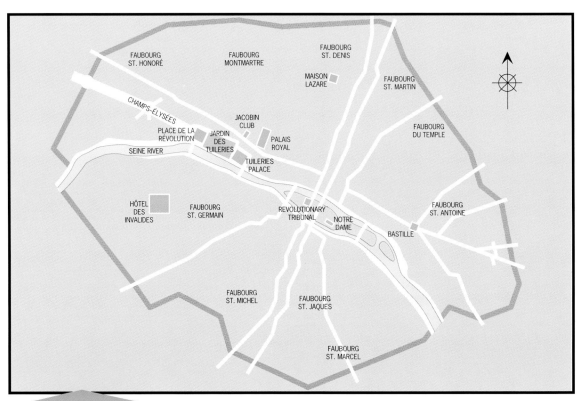

Paris in the time of the Revolution

To begin with, representatives of the mob tried negotiating with de Launay to give up the fortress. When nothing came of these talks, the crowd grew restless. Amid cries of "À nous la Bastille!" ("Give us the Bastille!"), a number of them forced their way through the outer courtyards toward the main drawbridge. De Launay ordered his troops to open fire on them, and 98 of the attackers were killed.

Lining up the cannons

By mid-afternoon, more anti-royalist soldiers had arrived in support of the mob. Among them were

veterans of the American Revolution, who took charge and lined up two cannons to fire at the drawbridge.

Realizing that all was probably lost, de Launay thought about setting off the gunpowder. Had he done so, the explosion would have blown up the Bastille and many surrounding streets. The men he commanded, not wanting to be blown to bits, prevented him from taking this course of action. Instead, the fortress surrendered.

De Launay's fate

As soon as the mob got inside the Bastille, they seized the gunpowder and set the prisoners free. Some of the victors were eager to take revenge on the soldiers who had fired on them. But others were able to calm them down, saving the lives of many in the defeated **garrison.** It was only de Launay and his officers who felt the full force of the people's anger. They were cruelly abused by the mob and then killed. DeLaunay's head was stuck on a spear and paraded through the streets of Paris.

It is interesting to compare this view of the Bastille under siege, made after it had been captured, with the more realistic one on page 18.

A FIGHT FOR ALL THE FAMILY

The fall of the Bastille was soon exaggerated into an heroic feat of arms by the citizens of Paris. The first edition of the newspaper *Révolutions de Paris,* published on July 17, 1789, described the attack on the Bastille as a sort of family day out, attended by wives, children, and grandparents:

"Women worked hard to support us, so did children. After every volley fired at us, the children ran around picking up the bullets and cannon balls. They then dodged back under cover and handed over what they had collected to our soldiers to fire back at the fortress."

The Revolution Saved

"It is a revolution"

On the evening of July 14, the king reportedly was told about the fall of the Bastille by the Duc de Rochefoucauld-Liancourt. *"Why, this is a revolt!"* Louis exclaimed. *"No, sire,"* the duke replied, *"it is a revolution."*

This was probably the first time Louis realized how serious the situation was. His army was crumbling, his government powerless. Once the mightiest king in Europe, he now appeared to have little more power than an ordinary citizen.

The king and the Assembly

The next morning Louis visited the Assembly at Versailles. There were no trumpets, **courtiers,** or guards. He came on foot and told the **deputies** that he had ordered his troops out of Paris. The Assembly was safe.

With a joyful crowd, the Marquis de Lafayette—a **veteran** of the American Revolution—carried the news to Paris. The city's royal government was replaced with a **Patriot** one and de Lafayette was put in charge of a new **militia.**

Although crowds hailed the king as a supporter of the revolution, members of the royal family knew better. On the night of July 16, one of the king's brothers and a group of his aristocrat friends fled Versailles for the border.

The Marquis de Lafayette was one of many French soldiers who had picked up revolutionary ideas while fighting in the American Revolution from 1775 to 1783.

King of a free people

On July 17, only three days after the fall of the Bastille, Louis traveled to Paris, accompanied by crowds of cheering citizens. Wearing simple clothes and riding in a plain coach, he made a triumphant entry into his capital. There he announced his new title: "Louis XVI, Father of the French, the King of a Free People."

Louis XVI, now "King of a Free People," arrives in Paris dressed as an ordinary citizen.

After publicly accepting the changes that had taken place, Louis appeared on a balcony before a delighted crowd. He was now just a powerless figurehead. Real power lay with the people of Paris. It was their colors—red and white—that Louis wore in a ribbon pinned to his hat.

THE DECLARATION OF THE RIGHTS OF MAN

On August 26, 1789, the National Assembly issued a *Declaration of the Rights of Man* that set out the principles of the new France. Two of its main articles were as follows:

Article 1. *"Men are born and remain free and equal in rights. Social distinctions may be based only upon the general good."*

Article 3. *"Sovereignty rests in the nation. No body or individual may exercise any authority which does not come directly from the nation."*

On from the Bastille

The Irish politician Edmund Burke (1729–1797) wrote a book called *Reflections on the Revolution in France* (1790) that was read all over Europe. It encouraged European rulers to resist the French Revolution.

Out of control

The events of July 12–14, 1789, marked a major turning point in the revolution. First, they showed how little power the king and his government actually had. Second, they united the **bourgeoisie** and the common people. Third, they gave the more extreme revolutionaries their first taste of blood.

After the fall of the Bastille and the king's visit to Paris, there was no turning back. But once the **Ancien Regime** had been abolished, there was disagreement over what should replace it.

Replacing the Ancien Regime

At first, France was guided by moderate reformers like de Lafayette and Honoré Mirabeau. The National Assembly abolished **nobles'** titles and **privileges,** set up a new legal system, took over the Church's land, and reorganized the country into 83 departments.

The Assembly also gave France a new **constitution,** which went into effect in 1791. A Legislative Assembly replaced the old National Assembly. The king could still refuse to allow new laws if he did not approve of them. Many officials, including members of the **clergy,** were elected. All fairly wealthy men, but no women, had a vote. So far, the revolution was exactly what the bourgeoisie had been wanting.

The flight to Varennes

In his heart, though, Louis XVI never accepted the revolution. On June 21, 1791, he and the royal family fled from Paris and made their way in disguise toward what is now known as Belgium. They were recognized at Varennes, near the border, and brought back to Paris. Louis had left behind a letter saying what he really thought of the revolution and, from then on, many saw him as a traitor.

Becoming a republic

The events in France horrified the monarchs of Europe, who feared that their own subjects might rise in revolt. In April 1792, Austria and Prussia declared war on France and invaded. The Prussian commander, the Duke of Brunswick, promised to restore the Ancien Regime. Louis XVI was an obstacle to the French war effort, but the Assembly refused to condemn him. Fearing that the invasion would lead to the end of the revolution, on August 10 the people of Paris stormed the National Assembly. There they forced the **deputies** to make France a **republic.**

The fate of those accused of being anti-revolutionary was settled by revolutionary committees such as this one, which were sometimes unfair.

The End of the Revolution

The death of the king

The revolution was getting more extreme and more violent. A **Convention,** made up mainly of the middle classes, replaced the Assembly in September 1792. In January 1793, it found Louis XVI guilty of **treason** and he was executed by **guillotine.** This started a "Reign of Terror" that lasted through July 1794. During the Terror, thousands of "enemies of the people"—**nobles, bourgeoisie,** priests, and others —were killed. Many more fled France to escape the violence.

"Behold the head of a traitor!" At the execution of Louis XVI, the guillotine was surrounded by soldiers, in case of trouble.

Jacobins and Girondists

Instead of concentrating on sorting out the new **republic,** the Convention soon became the scene of a bitter power struggle between different bourgeoisie groups.

The radical Jacobin party, led by Maximilien Robespierre, wanted France strictly governed to preserve the Revolution. It was the Jacobins who had called for the king's execution. Their opponents were the more moderate Girondists. The Jacobins got control of the Convention and the Convention's Committee of Public Safety that governed the country. They used the Reign of Terror to get rid of their opponents in the Girondist party.

Between March 1793 and April 1794 the victims of the guillotine were not only aristocrats and priests, but bourgeoisie and **peasants** too. It seemed the Revolution was making victims of its own supporters.

The slaughter spread to other parts of France. In Nantes, for example, thousands of opponents of the revolution were drowned in the Loire River. Following this, 100,000 more were killed in the war that broke out between Royalist and **Republican** supporters within the region of the Vendée, in the northwest of the country.

Insurrection against the Convention
Major centers of the Terror
Attacks by allied monarchist armies

BRITISH–DUTCH
ENGLAND
NETHERLANDS
Dunkerque
AUSTRIANS and PRUSSIANS
AUSTRIAN NETHERLANDS
Rouen
NORMANDY
Granville
PARIS
Varennes
BRITTANY
Rennes
Quiberon
Nantes
VENDÉE
Bourges
Dijon
BRITISH
SWISS CONFEDERATION
N
W E
S
Lyon
SAVOY
Bordeaux
PIEDMONT
Toulouse
Marseille
Toulon
SPAIN
BRITISH
miles 100
km 100

This map shows France from 1789 to 1794.

The Directory

Meanwhile France found itself at war with almost every other major European nation. Remarkably, the revolutionary army beat the invaders and advanced beyond French borders.

In July 1794, the Convention turned against Robespierre and his followers. They were removed from power and executed. The next year, a more moderate five-man council—the Directory—took over the government. It was in power until 1799, when it was overthrown by Napoleon Bonaparte. Napoleon's subsequent conquests spread France's revolutionary ideals across Europe.

THE REVOLUTIONARY CALENDAR

The French revolutionaries believed they were remaking the world. They instituted the metric system for weights, measures, and monetary units. They even changed the calendar. The new one had 12 months of 30 days each.

Bastille Day

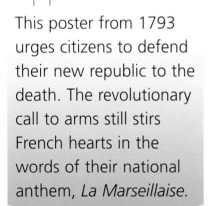

Why was it important?

The fall of the Bastille on July 14, 1789, is the most famous event of the entire French Revolution. A vast mythology soon grew up around the event. The prison was pictured as a huge fortress in which hundreds of prisoners were chained in damp and dingy dungeons. Its capture was described as a bloody battle marked by deeds of incredible courage.

But as we have seen, the old fortress was an unimportant prison that surrendered easily after unheroic fighting. So what made the fall of the Bastille so famous?

The new France

The importance of the fall of the Bastille was largely symbolic. The prison was important because it held critics of the **Ancien Regime** detained without trial by *lettres de cachet.* Its fall demonstrated the power of a group of ordinary people—shopkeepers, housewives, soldiers, servants—acting together.

The French Revolution and the rule of Napoleon changed France forever. Although the monarchy returned for a time, it was replaced by a **republic** in 1848. The **nobles'** power and **privilege** were reduced greatly. The Catholic Church also lost much of its wealth and influence. The new France was based upon liberty, equality, and brotherhood.

This poster from 1793 urges citizens to defend their new republic to the death. The revolutionary call to arms still stirs French hearts in the words of their national anthem, *La Marseillaise.*

The changes greatly helped the **bourgeoisie,** who gained control of the government. Only gradually did the benefits of the new regime filter down to the workers and **peasant** farmers.

Wider significance

French armies spread the ideals of the Enlightenment and the French Revolution over much of Europe. This made the fall of the Bastille significant for the whole continent. It marked the beginning of the end of the old Europe, controlled by all-powerful kings and emperors. In its place the modern, democratic Europe of today gradually began to emerge.

BASTILLE DAY

The Bastille story inspired the attack on the royal palace in 1792 and further French revolutions in 1830 and 1848. Not surprisingly, when in 1880 France established a National Day, it chose the anniversary of the fall of the Bastille—July 14. Bastille Day is still an annual holiday. It begins the traditional summer vacation season and is marked by parades, parties, speeches, and firework displays. As well as shouting *"Vive le 14 juillet!"* ("Long live the 14th of July!"), crowds also use the slogan first heard over 200 years ago: *"À bas la Bastille!"* ("Down with the Bastille!").

People in Paris celebrate Bastille Day with a parade.

Important Dates

1762		Rousseau's book *The Social Contract* is published
1774		Louis XVI becomes king
1775–1783		The American Revolution takes place
1786		Charles de Calonne presents his reforms to Louis XVI
1787		The Assembly of Notables meets
1789	**May 5**	The **Estates** General meets
	June 17	The Third Estate becomes the National Assembly
	June 20	The National Assembly swears the "tennis court" oath
	July 14	The Fall of the Bastille occurs
	August 26	The National Assembly agrees to the *Declaration of the Rights of Man*
1790		France is organized into 83 departments
		The law is reorganized
		Parlements are abolished
1791		The royal family flees Paris but is captured at Varennes
		The Legislative Assembly meets
1792		France goes to war with Austria and Prussia
		France is declared a **republic**
		De Lafayette flees the country
		French forces occupy the lands now known as Belgium
1793		Louis XVI is executed
		The Committee of Public Safety is set up in March to help run the country
		France goes to war with Britain, Holland, and Spain
		The "Reign of Terror" begins (ends in 1794)
1794		Robespierre is executed
1795		Louis XVII, son of Louis XVI, dies in prison
		The Directory is set up
1796–1797		Napoleon conquers Italy
1804		Napoleon is crowned emperor
1815		France restores the monarchy.
		Louis XVIII becomes king
1848		France becomes a republic again
1880		Bastille Day (July 14) becomes France's National Day

Glossary

Ancien Regime French society and government before the revolution, based on a rigid system of class and privilege

bankrupt having no money

bourgeoisie wealthy middle-class people

censorship suppression of certain facts in writing or other media

clergy group ordained as officials of the Catholic Church

constitution set of laws by which a country is governed

Convention type of congress called without the king's permission

courtier someone who serves or waits upon royalty

customs duty tax paid on goods entering and leaving a country

deputy someone chosen to represent the views of others

Estate one of the three groups (clergy, nobles, and common people) that made up society in the Ancien Regime

garrison military post

guillotine machine designed to behead people

heretic someone who disagrees with a teaching of the Church

Hôtel des Invalides military hospital in Paris that was sometimes used to house soldiers

inherited passed on from parent to child

interest fee that a borrower pays to someone who lends him or her money

livre main unit of French currency in the Ancien Regime

militia defense force

noble member of a privileged class of people next in importance to royalty

orator powerful public speaker

Parlement supreme law court of the Ancien Regime

Patriot someone who wanted the Ancien Regime to be reformed

peasant in Europe, a poor farmer

privilege rights, benefits, or favors granted to a person or group of people

radical favoring extreme change

republic country in which citizens elect representatives to run their government

republican in favor of a republic

servitude slavery

sou French coin with low value

treason crime of betraying one's country

tyranny cruel and often unlawful use of power and authority

veteran someone who has fought in a war

More Books to Read

Corzine, Phyllis. *The French Revolution.* San Diego, Calif.: Lucent Books, 1995.

Gilbert, Adrian. *The French Revolution.* Austin, Tex.: Raintree Steck-Vaughn Publishers, 1995.

Stewart, Gail B. *Life During the French Revolution.* San Diego, Calif.: Lucent Books, 1995.

Index